JUSTICE LEAGUE

THE ANIMATED SERIES GUIDE

LONDON, NEW YORK, MELBOURNE,
MUNICH, AND DELHI

Series Editor Alastair Dougall
Series Designer Robert Perry
Art Director Mark Richards
Publishing Manager Cynthia O'Neill Collins
Category Publisher Alex Kirkham
Production Claire Pearson
Dtp/Designer Dean Scholey

This title was designed and edited by Tall Tree Limited

First American Edition, 2004
04 05 06 07 10 9 8 7 6 5 4 3 2 1

Published in the United States by DK Publishing, Inc.
375 Hudson Street, New York, New York 10014

DK Publishing, Inc. offers special discounts for bulk purchases for sales promotions or premiums. Specific, large-quantity
needs can be met with special editions, including personalized covers, excerpts of existing guides, and corporate imprints.
For more information, contact Special Markets Department, DK Publishing, Inc., 375 Hudson Street, New York, NY 10014
Fax: 800-600-9098.

Library of Congress Cataloging-in-Publication Data

Hall, Jason.
  Justice League : the animated series guide / written by Jason Hall.--
1st American ed.
    p. cm. -- (The animated series guides)
  Includes index.
  ISBN 0-7566-0587-3 (PLC)
  1. Justice League (Television program)--Juvenile literature. 2. Justice
League of America (Fictitious characters)--Juvenile literature. I. Title.
II. Series.
  PN1992.77.J87H35 2004
  791.45'72--dc22

                        2004005004

Reproduced by Media Development and Printing, UK
Printed and bound in Italy by L.E.G.O.

Visit DC Comics online at www.dccomics.com or at keyword DC Comics on America Online.

see our complete product line at
www.dk.com

JUSTICE LEAGUE

THE ANIMATED SERIES GUIDE

Written by Jason Hall

DK

Contents

GREETINGS FROM THE WATCHTOWER

Welcome to the headquarters of the Justice League, the world's greatest heroes! The emergency alert sounds the moment that a world-threatening event appears on the Watchtower's monitors. Oh, no! The villainous Injustice Gang is breaking into S.T.A.R. Labs in Metropolis! Disaster! Starro's mind-controlled minions are attacking Tokyo! Help! A devastating earthquake has erupted in South America!

But never fear... Whether stopping a deadly alien invasion, protecting the planet from terrible natural disasters, or putting a dastardly super-villain behind bars, the Justice League is certain to save the day!

In its relentless fight for justice, this gallant band is duty bound to protect the innocent and fight evil. The world can be a dangerous place, but we can all sleep safer at night, thanks to the Justice League!

BAND OF SUPER HEROES

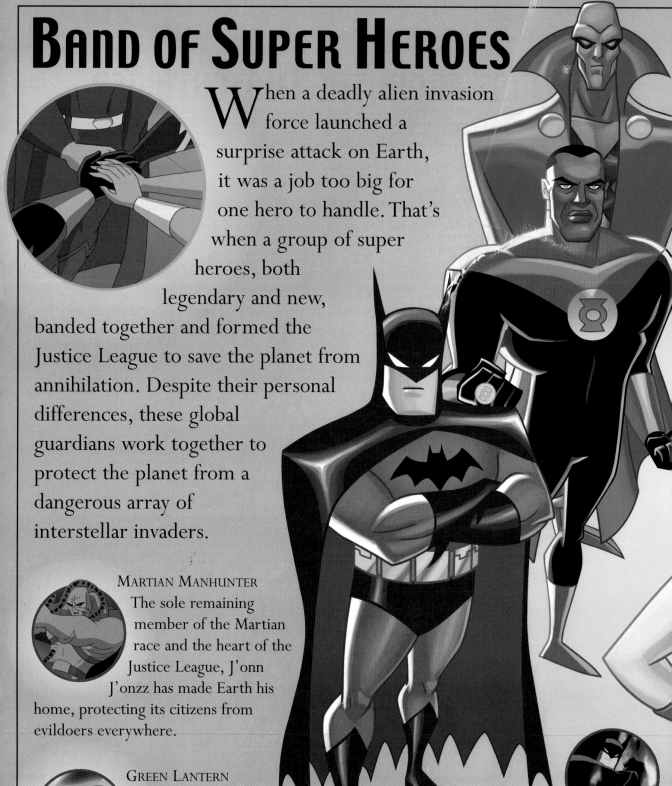

When a deadly alien invasion force launched a surprise attack on Earth, it was a job too big for one hero to handle. That's when a group of super heroes, both legendary and new, banded together and formed the Justice League to save the planet from annihilation. Despite their personal differences, these global guardians work together to protect the planet from a dangerous array of interstellar invaders.

MARTIAN MANHUNTER
The sole remaining member of the Martian race and the heart of the Justice League, J'onn J'onzz has made Earth his home, protecting its citizens from evildoers everywhere.

GREEN LANTERN
Armed with perhaps the mightiest weapon in the known universe, Green Lantern uses his power ring's emerald energy to accomplish the impossible.

BATMAN
Vowing never to let the tragedy of his parents' murder befall another innocent, Batman perfected his mind and body, transforming himself into the Dark Knight Detective.

THE FLASH
Granted unsurpassed superspeed, the Flash can take down a team of low-life criminals and crack three bad puns in the time it takes to blink.

HAWKGIRL
Accidentally transported from her home planet of Thanagar, Hawkgirl uses her detective skills and Thanagarian weapons to protect the people of Earth.

SUPERMAN
Rocketed from the dying planet Krypton and gifted with powers far beyond those of mortal men, Superman serves humankind as its greatest champion.

WONDER WOMAN
Once an Amazon princess, Wonder Woman now uses the powers given to her by the Greek gods to aid the Justice League in its battle against villainy.

SUPERMAN

Considered by many to be the Earth's greatest hero, the Man of Steel truly lives up to his legendary reputation. While his incredible superpowers derive from his home planet of Krypton, his unequalled moral strength comes from his simple upbringing in Kansas. Superman is the unofficial leader of the Justice League.

THANKS TO our solar system's yellow sun, Superman has tremendous superstrength. With the help of fellow JL member Green Lantern, the Last Son of Krypton was even able to move the Earth's moon!

A GIFT... A BURDEN

Clark Kent's powers became apparent at an early age, quickly making him a football star... and just as quickly ending his athletic career due to his unfair advantage over the other players.

JUSTICE DATA

• The one person Clark Kent cares most about is fellow reporter, Lois Lane. Too bad she only has eyes for his alter ego, Superman!

• Superman's Kryptonian name is "Kal-El." His Earth name, "Clark," was taken from Ma Kent's maiden name.

LUNGS OF STEEL

Superman's amazing cold breath can freeze criminals in their tracks and even stop tidal waves! The Man of Steel can also hold his breath for hours on end if necessary.

LOOK! UP IN THE SKY!

Thanks to the Earth's lighter gravity, Superman has the amazing power of flight. However, some "passengers" may prefer to keep their feet firmly on the ground!

WHILE SUPERMAN'S heat vision can melt through practically any substance, his X-ray vision allows him to see through any material, except lead. Utilizing his mighty "power clap" to create a sonic boom, Superman can literally shake his opponents down to their very atoms!

ALTHOUGH HE seems invulnerable, Superman can still be injured. Magic and electricity will throw him for a loop, and exposure to green kryptonite can take away his powers and even kill him.

BATMAN

When young Bruce Wayne witnessed the murder of his parents, he vowed to spend his life fighting crime. After years of training, Bruce donned the cape and cowl of the Batman to become Gotham's guardian. Although he has no superpowers of his own, Batman is often the key to the JL's victories.

AGAINST ALL ODDS

Batman often finds himself outnumbered by his enemies—and the odds stacked against him. But thanks to his expertly honed fighting skills, he always manages to come out on top!

THE ULTIMATE LONER, Batman prefers working in the shadows and shuns the limelight of the Justice League. But his teammates know they can count on him to be there when they need him.

JUSTICE DATA

• Batman is a part-time member of the League, but his colleagues want him to be a permanent fixture.

THOSE LONG GOTHAM NIGHTS

With so many roguish distractions in Gotham City, Batman must split his time between League membership and patrolling his home turf. So much for sleep!

BATMAN IS VERY secretive and likes to do things his own way, which sometimes puts him at odds with Superman's leadership. But despite their very different methods, saving lives always comes first.

DARK KNIGHT DETECTIVE

Possessing the keenest of analytical minds, Batman is truly the World's Greatest Detective. Many a crime has been solved thanks to the Dark Knight expertly piecing together a jigsaw of clues.

BATMAN HAS AMASSED an impressive arsenal of weapons to aid his war on crime. He can swing through the streets of Gotham with this bat-grapple and also use it to tie up crooks securely.

WONDER WOMAN

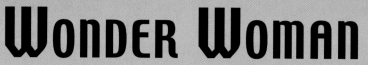

The daughter of the Queen of the Amazons, Princess Diana was born and raised on the legendary island of Themyscira. She was blessed by the gods with remarkable powers and trained by her Amazon sisters to be the ultimate warrior. As Wonder Woman, she heroically ventured out into the world to aid humankind.

WONDER WOMAN'S Golden Lasso was spun from the girdle of the Earth goddess Gaea and forged by the Greek god Hephaestus. With the Lasso's indestructible might, Wonder Woman can bind even the most monstrous of metallic marauders!

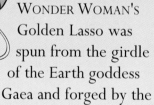

BULLETS AND BRACELETS

Wonder Woman can deflect a barrage of bullets with her silver bracelets, crafted from the shield of Zeus himself. The bracelets are not only a formidable defensive weapon, but also a symbol of the imprisonment the Amazons endured at the hands of Heracles ages ago.

MIGHTY GIFTS

Wonder Woman's powers were bestowed on her by the Greek gods. As well as the power of flight, she was given speed and strength, great wisdom, the eye of a hunter, a unity with nature, and a loving heart.

- Princess Diana was sculpted from clay by her mother. She was then made flesh and brought to life by the gods of Mount Olympus.

- Wonder Woman's uniform is actually the sacred armor of the Amazons!

MOTHER'S LITTLE GIRL

Although Diana left Themyscira against her mother's wishes, Hippolyta still keeps a worried eye on her daring daughter. While proud of Diana's accomplishments with the Justice League, the Amazon Queen wishes to keep her island paradise untainted by the influence of Man's World.

ARES, GOD OF WAR

Eager to create conflict for its own sake, Wonder Woman's nemesis, Ares, impersonated the goddess Athena in an attempt to turn the Amazons against the outside world. However, Wonder Woman and the Justice League managed to put a stop to Ares's evil plans.

HAWKGIRL

While pursuing a gang of criminals on her native planet of Thanagar, police detective Shayera Hol was zapped by a dimensional transport beam and sent halfway across the galaxy to Earth. Choosing the guise of Hawkgirl, she uses her native powers to protect her adoptive planet, hoping one day to return home.

HAWKGIRL CAN give Batman a run for his money in the super-sleuthing department! As a trained detective, her powers of observation impress even the Dark Knight Detective himself.

The Thanagarian energy mace is Hawkgirl's weapon of choice.

FEARLESS FIGHTER

Warlike, but with an air of exotic mystery, Hawkgirl never backs down from a fight. Although she has revealed very little about her distant homeworld, one can't help but wonder if her battle-born nature doesn't stem from her Thanagarian heritage.

BAM

Graceful wings are this Thanagarian's birthright, enabling her to soar through the air with astonishing agility.

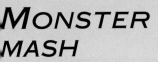

MONSTER MASH

Hawkgirl's training as a Thanagarian police officer makes her a formidable hand-to-hand combatant, as well as an expert with a variety of alien weapons. With a mighty battle-cry, she expertly brandishes her energy mace, taking down evildoers with one mighty blow.

HAWKGIRL IS sometimes put off by Wonder Woman's regal manner, but it required the mind-controlling powers of the alien Dominators to put the women of the Justice League at each other's throats.

ANCIENT INSPIRATION

When she's not solving crimes with the Justice League, Shayera enjoys taking in the Egyptian exhibits at the Midway City Museum. Ancient legends of hawklike gods are fascinating to this winged wonder.

JUSTICE DATA

• Hawkgirl's wings aren't mechanical, but an organic part of her body.

• Hawkgirl has developed a romance with fellow team member Green Lantern.

GREEN LANTERN

Recognized by the Guardians of Oa for having extraordinary courage and heroism, John Stewart was awarded a power ring and trained to be a member of the Green Lantern Corps. After years of patrolling the deepest reaches of space, John has returned home to protect Earth as a member of the Justice League.

GREEN LANTERN'S ring is an incredible weapon wielded simply by the power of thought. It is able to project powerful energy beams, impenetrable force fields, and amazing constructs limited only by the wearer's imagination. Its emerald aura also protects Green Lantern from the harsh environs of space.

Green Lantern uses his ring to project an impenetrable energy shield about him.

LORD OF THE RING

John Stewart is an expert ring-slinger! Through sheer will power, the Emerald Knight can use his ring to stop a building from collapsing and even protect a city from an oncoming tidal wave!

JUSTICE DATA

- Green Lantern's power ring must be recharged every 24 hours from a lanternlike power battery.

- While John Stewart was patrolling deep space, *Daily Planet* artist Kyle Rayner temporarily became Earth's Green Lantern, battling the evil Sinestro.

EVEN THOUGH John enjoys spending his few spare moments back in his old neighborhood, his Green Lantern persona is always with him. He's worn his ring for so long that its green energy has infused his entire being!

JUST ONE OF THE GANG

John is simply one of many Green Lanterns that comprise the elite Green Lantern Corps—the intergalactic peacekeeping force created by the Guardians of Oa. Its heroic ranks are filled with diverse aliens from across the galaxy.

FALLEN FRIENDS

The life of a Green Lantern is perilous, and John has seen many comrades fall in the line of duty. But their deaths only strengthen GL's resolve to protect the galaxy.

THE FLASH

Thanks to a freak electro-chemical accident, Wally West gained the power of superspeed, becoming the Flash—the fastest man alive. As the youngest member of the League, the brash Flash has a quick wit and a light-hearted view of danger. But he often acts on impulse without considering the consequences.

NEED SPEED

With the ability to run at nearly the speed of light, defying gravity and matching the velocity of sound is a walk in the park for the Flash. Even Superman has a hard time keeping up with the Scarlet Speedster!

THE FLASH moves so quickly, it can almost seem as if he's in three places at once. And the Justice League thought even one Flash was more than enough to handle!

A MATTER OF TIME

With the help of the Cosmic Treadmill, the Atom's technological wonder, the Flash can use his incredible speed to travel through time— allowing him to save the day in any century!

With the ability to move so fast, the Flash has even found the right frequency to transform himself into radio waves!

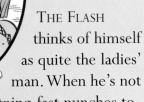

THE FLASH thinks of himself as quite the ladies' man. When he's not delivering lightning-fast punches to Captain Cold or Mirror Master, you can find Wally at the nearest nightclub, flirting up a storm!

JUSTICE DATA

• As the youngest member of the Justice League, the Flash often comes across as a bit immature. Sometimes the other members just wish he'd grow up!

• Because of his super-fast metabolism, the Flash is constantly hungry. He can pack away more hamburgers than an entire pro-football team!

THE FLASH'S WEAKNESS for a beautiful woman can also put him in a bind… like the time the Amazonian villain Aresia managed to slap the cuffs on Wally and make a quick getaway.

MARTIAN MANHUNTER

J'onn J'onzz, the last survivor of an ancient Martian race, traveled to Earth warning of an impending alien invasion. Although met with hostility at first, J'onn helped repel the evil space marauders alongside the heroes that became the mighty Justice League.

REALIZING THAT that Earthlings fear the unusual, J'onn uses his shape-shifting abilities to maintain his more humanlike Martian Manhunter appearance. However, he sometimes reverts to his true Martian form in moments of quiet solitude or when attacked.

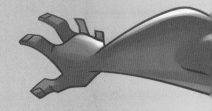

INTO AIR

Enemies find it difficult to land a punch on the Martian Manhunter! With the power to alter his physical density, J'onn can become immaterial and even pass through solid objects.

JUSTICE DATA

• Fascinated by the human race, J'onn sometimes uses his shape-shifting ability to walk secretly among us and observe human behavior.

• J'onn can be weakened by exposure to intense heat.

DOUBLE TROUBLE

When the annihilators of his race threatened to return to Earth, J'onn found they had planted an impostor in the League. However, he was shocked to discover that the spy was in fact himself! The aliens had transferred the real Manhunter's memories to a shape-shifting agent.

J'onn's most amazing Martian power is telepathy. He can read the minds of others and even communicate with his fellow Leaguers simply by projecting his thoughts!

J'onn's body can transform from solid mass to mist in a matter of seconds.

BESIDES GREAT strength and the power of flight, J'onn possesses the natural Martian ability to change his shape, allowing him to take the form of anyone he chooses!

MIND OVER MATTER

When his telepathy wasn't enough to penetrate the thoughts of potentially hostile aliens, J'onn used an amplifier helmet powered by Green Lantern's ring to get the job done.

Green Lantern's ring gives J'onn enough power to read even the most opaque alien minds.

THE WATCHTOWER

Floating in geo-synchronous orbit around the Earth is the Justice League's space station headquarters, the Watchtower. This high-tech monitoring station acts as an early warning system for threats coming from the far reaches of outer space. It also looks out for trouble on remote corners of the planet.

WHETHER planning a strategy to stop Lex Luthor or debriefing after a clash with Gorilla Grodd, the Round Table is where the members of the Justice League meet to discuss their astounding adventures. Each seat at the table is designated by a member's particular emblem.

The Watchtower is well protected by an array of shields and defense systems.

HOME IMPROVEMENTS

In an attempt to increase the range of the Justice League Emergency Signal, Superman and Green Lantern attached a more powerful transmitter relay onto the Watchtower's outer hull. Not your usual trip to the hardware store!

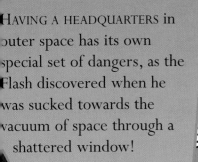

HAVING A HEADQUARTERS in outer space has its own special set of dangers, as the Flash discovered when he was sucked towards the vacuum of space through a shattered window!

ON VIEW

The view from the Watchtower is breathtaking, with its panoramic "spacescape" vistas providing the ideal atmosphere for deep contemplation. How many heroes can say they have a great view of Earth from their office window?

WATCH ROOM

The Watchtower's monitor room is outfitted with viewing screens and state-of-the-art telecommunications. Each League member takes a turn at monitor duty, keeping an eye out for any potential threats to Earth's safety.

THE JUSTICE League's transport, the *Javelin-7*, is housed in an enormous hangar equipped with all the tools necessary to keep the impressive ship running smoothly.

JUSTICE DATA

• The Watchtower was secretly financed by Batman, using funds from Wayne Technologies.

• Although the Watchtower has living space, the Martian Manhunter is the only member to live there full time.

Vehicles and Gadgets

Even though the Justice League is comprised of the Earth's mightiest heroes, the team sometimes needs a helping hand from modern technology. An assortment of high-tech gadgets and gizmos is at their disposal—and anything not on hand can be constructed in the Watchtower's lab.

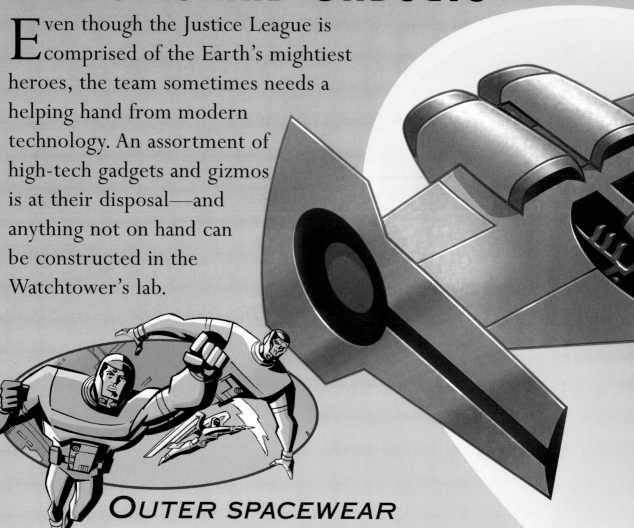

Outer spacewear

While Green Lantern can use his power ring to survive the freezing depths of space, the other members of the League rely on the latest protective space suits when a mission takes them beyond the Earth's atmosphere.

When the Justice League needed to create an artificial moon, they turned to science for the solution. Utilizing the Watchtower's ultra-advanced laboratory (and J'onn J'onzz's Martian mathematics), the Flash managed to whip up an artificial-gravity device!

Justice Data

• The Justice League comm link doubles as an emergency signal device.

• In the fight for justice, the team is sometimes able to make use of a villain's weapon from the Watchtower trophy room!

DRIVING IN STYLE

Each Justice League member is trained to pilot the team's ultra-advanced shuttle, the *Javelin-7*. This remarkable craft is used to transport the heroes to and from the Watchtower, as well as take them on missions throughout the galaxy.

The Javelin-7's shatterproof cockpit glass can even withstand meteorite impacts!

BAT-TECH

No hero has a cache of personal weapons greater than Batman's! Between his Batarang, Bat-bolo, Bat-grapple, and the missile-armed Batwing, the Dark Knight has a "Bat-device" for almost any emergency that may arise.

Batarang

Bat-bolo

The craft's turbo impellers drive the two ion engines at the rear, providing incredible thrust.

LINES OF COMMUNICATION

Remaining in constant contact is an important factor for any team. But with the wide transmitting range of the Justice League comm link, each hero is just a call away.

AQUAMAN

King of Atlantis and protector of the seven seas, Aquaman was born with the ability to communicate telepathically with all the creatures of the ocean. Aquaman will safeguard his kingdom at any cost, even if it means clashing with surface-world dwellers or the heroes of the Justice League!

NOT ONLY can Aquaman "talk to fish," he can mentally converse with any of the animals beneath the ocean's waves. Whether they're dolphins, whales, sharks, jellyfish, or even giant squid, the seafaring champion can ask them for assistance in times of need.

A FATHER'S SACRIFICE

In order to free himself and save the life of his infant son, Aquaman selflessly cut off his own left hand! Now his entire hand has been replaced with a deadly harpoon that can be fired and retracted like a grappling hook.

JUSTICE DATA

• Aquaman rules Atlantis with Mera, his beautiful, strong-willed wife, at his side.

• Aquaman is resentful of the surface dwellers' blatant disregard for the ecology of his beloved oceans, though recently he has negotiated a peace treaty with the United Nations.

Besides his aquatic telepathy, Aquaman can both breathe and talk underwater! Because his body is accustomed to living in the ocean's depths, he also possesses exceedingly strong skin.

PRETTY POISON

The Justice League thought Aquaman had turned rogue when he commanded a horde of sea-creatures to attack the shores of Gotham City. Little did the heroes know that their aquatic ally was under the control of Poison Ivy's toxic touch!

THANKS TO the Martian Manhunter's perfect impersonation of Aquaman, the League managed to take the botanical beauty by surprise!

ONCE FREED from Ivy's venomous manipulation, it was time to teach her a lesson! While her plans to protect plant-life may mirror Aquaman's desire to safeguard the seas, the Atlantian king made sure she knew her villainous means were far from justified.

THE ATOM

Using a fragment of a white dwarf star that had fallen to Earth, Professor Ray Palmer created a costume and controls that enabled him to shrink to microscopic size. As the Atom, he bravely lends the Justice League a hand whenever they need a little help with a big crisis!

NOT CONTENT WITH being able to shrink himself, the Atom has also shrunk most of the Justice League. He did this in order to battle an alien commando team that had entered Superman's body and were about to take control of the Man of Steel!

THE ATOM often teams up with his buddy, the Flash. Once, the two used the time-traveling Cosmic Treadmill to stop the criminal Chronos from tampering with the time-stream.

MIGHTY MITE

In spite of his small stature, the Atom still packs a wallop! Even when he's miniaturized, the Tiny Titan retains his full-size strength.

JUSTICE DATA

• The planet Rann is made up of city-states that vary from scientifically advanced to barbarically primitive.

• When he's not out adventuring, Professor Palmer teaches physics at Ivy University.

ADAM STRANGE

While fleeing for his life from savage South American natives, treasure-hunting archeologist Adam Strange was zapped by a Zeta Beam sent from the planet Rann. Although designed to communicate with Earth, the beam was altered by its journey through space and somehow teleported Adam light years away to its planet of origin!

ALIEN DESTINY

Strange became the planet's champion and protector, defending its people from all kinds of dangerous threats—like this colossal reptilian beast!

THE CAPITAL CITY of Rann is Ranagar, a great metropolis of futuristic technology and wonder. This is where Adam met Sardath, chief of Rann's science counsel.

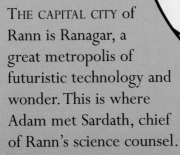

STAR ROMANCE

Adventure wasn't the only thing Adam found across the stars! He also discovered true love with Sardath's beautiful and enchanting daughter, Alanna. Their feelings for each other compeled Adam to propose marriage to Alanna and make his home on Rann.

LEX LUTHOR

With his lifetime of criminal dealings finally uncovered, Lex Luthor can no longer strike at his enemies under the guise of a successful businessman. But this manipulative mastermind is still one of the most dangerous men on the planet! Driven mad by kryptonite poisoning, Luthor has turned his genius and vast personal fortune to one end: destroying Superman and the Justice League.

LUTHOR HAD a genius for creating alibis that concealed his illicit activities. But now that the public knows he's operating on the wrong side of the law, Lex doesn't worry about hiding his ulterior motives.

JUSTICE DATA

• Lex's high-tech armor not only packs enough power to take on the entire Justice League, but also helps slow the spread of his kryptonite poisoning.

• After helping the JL deal with a threat from an alternate timeline, Lex was granted a pardon for his crimes and has turned to politics.

LUXURY LOST

Luthor's luxurious lifestyle is a thing of the past. Once his true colors were revealed, Lex went from brokering multi-million-dollar deals in a tropical paradise to devising escape plans from a prison cell.

LUTHOR LAB

Since becoming a career criminal, Luthor has started flexing his scientific genius. His cunning master plans are now devised in a science lab, not a boardroom.

FALLING INTO MADNESS

Luthor's obsession with destroying the Man of Steel finally took its toll. Over the years, repeated exposure to kryptonite's low-level radioactivity caused Luthor to contract kryptonite poisoning. As a result, Lex's steel-trap mind became more and more unstable.

MOVING UP

Even though Lex Luthor was finally brought to justice, his multi-billion-dollar company continued to thrive without him. Mercy Graves, Luthor's former chauffeur, became the new chief executive of LexCorp in his absence. Talk about a promotion!

LUTHOR OCCASIONALLY teams up with other well-known criminals. He once secretly partnered the Joker in an attempt to kill Superman, and formed the Injustice Gang to exact revenge upon the Justice League.

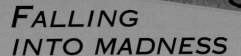

THE INJUSTICE GANG

Just as the heroes of the Justice League teamed up for the greater good, a host of vile villains did the same in order to further their own insane agendas. Originally formed by Lex Luthor, the Injustice Gang is easily one of the JL's deadliest adversaries.

THE ULTRA-HUMANITE was once a human scientist who transplanted his over-sized brain into the body of a gorilla. A cultured mastermind, this simian super-genius has more class than your average super-villain.

POSSESSING A menacing gothic persona, the Shade can trap any foe in an inky black void emitted from his walking cane. These sentient shadows plunge victims into total darkness and are ideal for masking any entry or escape.

SWAMP BORN

Evil Cyrus Gold was gunned down and cursed by his criminal associates. His body was then thrown into a swamp that possessed magical properties. Decades later, the swamp gave birth to Solomon Grundy—a walking dead man, soulless and empty.

Like Green Lantern's power ring, Star Sapphire's deadly gem is thought-activated.

JUSTICE DATA

- Other members of the Injustice Gang have included Cheetah (right), the Joker, and Tsukuri.

STAR SAPPHIRE

Suffering from a split personality due to a psychotic breakdown, this vicious vixen possesses a power gem that allows her to fly. It also shoots deadly fuchsia energy blasts similar to those fired by Green Lantern's power ring.

ARESIA

The orphaned Aresia was raised by the Amazons and gained their strength and agility. But this did little to quench her thirst for vengeance against men, whom she blamed for the death of her family. She reformed the Injustice Gang to her aid in her plans for revenge.

Aresia's legendary charms once captivated the men of the JL, and drove them to do her every bidding.

COPPERHEAD IS A venomous villain whose sole motivation is money. He has considerable strength and agility, a prehensile tail, can scale walls, and has a headpiece with poisonous fangs. His snakelike tongue is quick to slither, which suggests he is perhaps something more than human.

33

PSYCHO-PIRATE

Roger Hayden was a talented psychiatrist suspended for malpractice after he became addicted to the emotional distress of his patients. When his wife and son were killed during a battle between the JL and alien invaders, Hayden's mind snapped. The disturbed doctor transformed into one of the League's most mind-blowing menaces —the emotion-manipulating Psycho-Pirate!

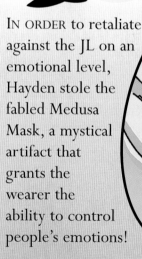

IN ORDER to retaliate against the JL on an emotional level, Hayden stole the fabled Medusa Mask, a mystical artifact that grants the wearer the ability to control people's emotions!

DERANGED THERAPY

Hayden blamed the Justice League for his family's demise, displacing his own feelings of tremendous guilt concerning their fate. Determined to destroy the heroes any way he could, he looked for a magically powerful means to carry out his revenge.

EMOTIONAL BAGGAGE

With the might of the mask at his disposal, Hayden took on the guise of the Psycho-Pirate, relishing his newfound power. By driving people's emotions out of control, it was child's play to turn the people against their heroes.

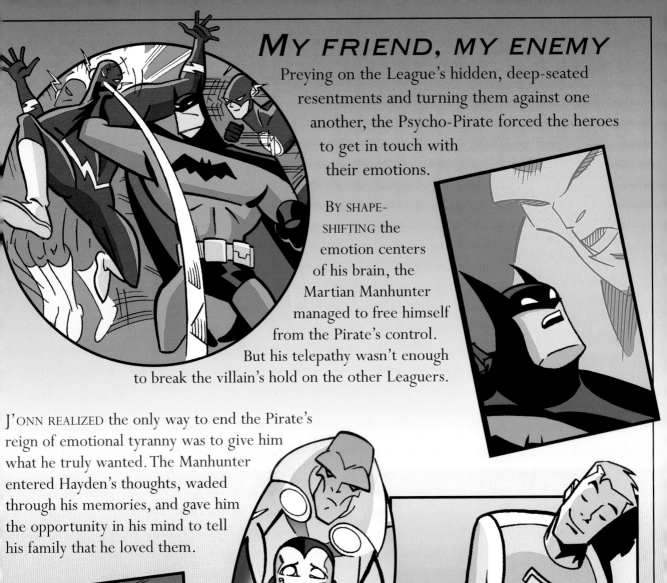

MY FRIEND, MY ENEMY

Preying on the League's hidden, deep-seated resentments and turning them against one another, the Psycho-Pirate forced the heroes to get in touch with their emotions.

BY SHAPE-SHIFTING the emotion centers of his brain, the Martian Manhunter managed to free himself from the Pirate's control. But his telepathy wasn't enough to break the villain's hold on the other Leaguers.

J'ONN REALIZED the only way to end the Pirate's reign of emotional tyranny was to give him what he truly wanted. The Manhunter entered Hayden's thoughts, waded through his memories, and gave him the opportunity in his mind to tell his family that he loved them.

JUSTICE DATA

• The Medusa Mask was donated to the Midway City Museum by Kent Nelson, who has teamed up with the Justice League as the Lord of Order, Dr. Fate!

• After their brush with the Psycho-Pirate, the JL took a vacation together to help them come to terms with their differences and remain an effective team.

THE COLD WARRIORS

This gathering of frosty foes is enough to put a chill in any super hero's bones! Claiming to have taken over the drought-stricken country of Bijouti to provide relief, these rogues threatened a "cold war" unless the United Nations provided ten billion dollars in aid. But there was an ulterior motive to the Cold Warriors' supposedly warm intentions.

Captain Cold and Cryonic Man

Killer Frost

Mr. Freeze

Polar Lord

Snowman

Minister Blizzard and Icicle

WHEN THE Justice League arrived to liberate the citizens of Bijouti from their icy new dictators, they received a chilly welcome. The Cold Warriors had actually supplied the deprived people with much-needed food and clothes. Little did the people know that the provisions were stolen from other UN relief missions!

AFTER A LITTLE super-sleuthing, the League discovered that Polar Lord was really General Eklu, a renegade from the planet Tharr who was preparing the Earth for invasion! He had recruited the Warriors to help rule his new cold order.

ARCTIC ARSENAL

The heroes' efforts to shut down Eklu's icebot factory were met with ice-cold resistance, as an army of the robotic soldiers retaliated in full force! But when the mechanical monsters reacted to the League's attack as if in pain, a quick scan with the Martian Manhunter's telepathy revealed that the people of Bijouti were inside!

THE BIJOUTI people weren't the only victims of a double-cross. Eklu had all the Cold Warriors on ice, using them as bait to lure the Justice League into his trap. The only way the League could defeat Eklu's Tharrian army was by freeing the Warriors, who were more than eager to turn the tables on their former ally.

SUPERMAN AND Green Lantern reversed the country's sub-zero climate by creating a greenhouse effect. This not only melted the ice, but also created enough moisture to bring desperately needed rains.

JUSTICE DATA

• Mr. Freeze is one of Batman's arch-enemies, while Captain Cold tends to give the Flash the runaround whenever possible.

CHRONOS

After spending plenty of time behind bars, petty crook David Clinton decided he needed time on his side. Stealing and developing time-travel technology, Clinton became Chronos the Time-Thief! Too bad for him that history tends to repeat itself, as the Justice League always puts a stop to his evil escapades.

TIME TALE

In an attempt to save the life of his brother Bobby, the aged Chronos of the future traveled through time and warned his younger self of Bobby's imminent death.

HOWEVER, MUCKING with time can lead to serious headaches! After each failed attempt to save his brother, Chronos sent another of his selves back in time to try again, further weakening the time-stream.

CHRONOS FINALLY realized the error of his ways when he saw his brother face to face the moment before the young man died. Bobby had willingly sacrificed his life to save others from a fire, and it wasn't right for Chronos to change that past.

JUSTICE DATA

• In an elaborate ruse to catch the League's deadliest enemies, Batman once impersonated Chronos, pretending to auction off captured members of the League to the highest bidder!

KOBRA

The eyes on Kobra's snake staff glow red before it fires a lethal energy blast.

With the mindless minions of the Kobra Cult at his beck and call, the super-terrorist Kobra will stop at nothing to achieve global domination. This self-proclaimed King of Serpents believes he is a snake-god in human form whose destiny is to rule the world!

SNAKE'S BITE

Kobra's weapon is a staff shaped like a giant king cobra, capable of firing powerful energy blasts. Just as deadly is this cold-blooded killer's second-in-command, Lady Eve, who has treacherous plans of her own to take over the Kobra Cult!

BZAKT!

KOBRA'S PERSUASIVE forked tongue easily convinces his disciples to follow him blindly. The cold-blooded killer's loyal supporters will do anything for their diabolical leader, even if it means going head-to-head with the mighty Justice League!

IN HIS FINAL ASSAULT, Kobra launched missiles containing a lethal nerve gas. But thanks to skilled teamwork, the Justice League managed to destroy the weapons before the gas could be released, leaving Kobra with a one-way ticket to prison.

STARRO

Many of the League's deadliest adversaries are out of this world! With its millions of parasitic offspring, the starfish-shaped Starro has an insatiable hunger to take over planets. This queen's brood of Star Conquerors attach themselves to a planet's people, subjugate their will, and drain the life-force from them.

FIRST CONTACT

When a spaceship crashed in Wisconsin, the Justice League found that all inside had energy-sucking starfish attached to their faces! The heroes learned from the sole survivor that Starro had decimated his planet and was planning to target Earth next!

THE JUSTICE LEAGUE journeyed to the survivor's homeworld to face Starro's minions, but were quickly overwhelmed by the sheer number of mind-controlling aliens.

SOUL SURVIVOR

The Flash managed to make a quick escape and discovered Godunn, the last survivor of a Green Lantern unit that had attempted to stop the Star Conquerors.

ONCE FLASH and Godunn had managed to free the League from their mental enslavement, the heroes used every ounce of their strength to keep Starro's great eye from opening a portal to Earth.

IN A LAST DITCH attempt to stop Starro, Hawkgirl flew the *Javelin-7* into the creature's giant eye. The impact weakened the alien queen and transported the entire Justice League safely back to Earth's orbit.

THE FINAL blow came from Godunn, who valiantly sacrificed himself to destroy the injured Starro and its litter of starfish creatures!

JUSTICE DATA

• The threat of the Star Conquerors would return again in 50 years' time to trouble Superman and the Justice League Unlimited!

• Starro weakens its victims by giving them peaceful mental dreams of becoming one with its collective of Star Conquerors.

ALIEN INVADERS 1

It seems that Earth is quite a popular target for intergalactic armies! Whether defending the planet from hordes of space invaders or traveling through the galaxy to face an alien threat head-on, the Justice League has battled with the very worst the universe has to offer.

AFTER BEING FREED accidentally from their prison on Mars, the "Martian killers" launched an armada against Earth. Armed with laser rifles and attack ships, and possessing shape-shifting abilities, these aliens planned to assimilate the human race.

THE ANTAREANS have developed what they consider to be a more "civilized" form of warfare. Each of their three civilizations may engage in battle with the other two only according to strict traditions of war. The combatants believe this allows them to fight without savagery.

A PETTY SPACE PIRATE and smuggler, Kanjar Ro was once hired by the Manhunters to help frame Green Lantern for the destruction of an entire planet.

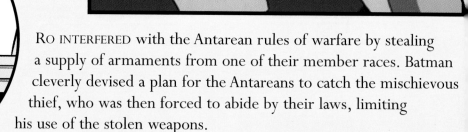

RO INTERFERED with the Antarean rules of warfare by stealing a supply of armaments from one of their member races. Batman cleverly devised a plan for the Antareans to catch the mischievous thief, who was then forced to abide by their laws, limiting his use of the stolen weapons.

- Only sunlight can stop the "Martian killers."

- The Dominators will return to cause trouble for a team of future super heroes inspired by the Justice League: the Legion of Super Heroes!

WHEN THE FLASH accidentally became two-dimensional, he discovered an army of 2-D aliens threatening to overrun our three-dimensional world. But the Scarlet Speedster was able to turn the tables on them, trapping them in a one-dimensional universe!

Dominators belonging to the highest castes are more cruel than the rest of their race.

THE TELEPATHIC Dominators consider themselves superior to all other alien races, and have no qualms about experimenting on "lesser beings." Their society is divided into castes, where status is designated by the size of a disk worn on the forehead.

ALIEN INVADERS 2

Not all alien visitors have malicious intentions. Sometimes these extraterrestrials are simply misunderstood or misguided. Although they may appear hostile at first, many end up as allies or even friends in the end.

ANSWERING A distress signal from a damaged Space Ark, the Justice League discovered only four survivors: freedom fighters from the planet Daxam. These alien refugees soon discovered that under Earth's yellow sun they had the same abilities as Superman! With their newfound powers, the Daxamites began a quest to end all war and suffering on the planet. But when their efforts proved more harmful than helpful, the League taught them not to abuse power in the fight for what is right.

JUSTICE DATA

• The Justice League has a number of alien allies and friends, including Orion and Highfather of New Genesis.

WHEN ENORMOUS SEA waves threatened imminent destruction around the globe, the Justice League was quick to stem the tide. But these natural disasters were only a symptom of a much larger, and surprising, problem…

BABY ON BOARD

Realizing that the tidal waves must have been caused by an abnormal gravitational pull from the moon, the League took a closer look and was shocked to discover an unborn alien being inside! The heroes created an artificial moon to temporarily replace the original, allowing the alien creature to "hatch" without further threat to Earth.

THE SHAYOL'S attempt to contact Earth in peace was misconstrued as an attack. This was perhaps not surprising, as their former rulers had killed members of the Green Lantern Corps! Once the Justice League established contact, however, the Shayol's true intentions were brought to light.

MICROSCOPIC ALIEN frogmen infiltrated Earth to bring revenge against a foe named "Evano the Terrible." This human had drowned the crew of their exploration vehicle. However, the frogmen soon learned their mortal enemy was in fact a man named Evan Offenhauser who, as a child, had found their tiny ship. Thinking it was a toy, he played with it in the bathtub!

The microscopic frogmen were put at the mercy of a child when their miniature machine was manhandled!

GAZETTEER

The 2-D Aliens first appeared in FLASH FAX (JUSTICE LEAGUE ADVENTURES #7).

Adam Strange first appeared in STRANGE DAYS, Part One (JUSTICE LEAGUE ADVENTURES #25).

The Alien Invaders first appeared in SECRET ORIGINS, Part One (Episode #1).

Aquaman first appeared on JUSTICE LEAGUE in THE ENEMY BELOW, Part One (Episode #6).

The Antareans first appeared in ENSLAVED! (JUSTICE LEAGUE ADVENTURES #15).

Aresia first appeared in FURY, Part One (Episode #16).

Ares first appeared in WORLD WAR OF THE SEXES (JUSTICE LEAGUE ADVENTURES #4).

The Atom first appeared in THE MOMENT (JUSTICE LEAGUE ADVENTURES #11).

Batman first appeared on JUSTICE LEAGUE in SECRET ORIGINS, Part One (Episode #1).

Captain Cold first appeared in WOLF'S CLOTHING (JUSTICE LEAGUE ADVENTURES #6).

Chronos first appeared in WOLF'S CLOTHING (JUSTICE LEAGUE ADVENTURES #6).

Copperhead first appeared in INJUSTICE FOR ALL, Part One (Episode #8).

Cryonic Man first appeared in COLD WAR (JUSTICE LEAGUE ADVENTURES #12).

The Daxamites first appeared in THE STAR LOST (JUSTICE LEAGUE ADVENTURES #3).

Dr. Fate first appeared on JUSTICE LEAGUE in THE TERROR BEYOND, Part One (Episode #39).

The Dominators first appeared in SANCTUARY (JUSTICE LEAGUE ADVENTURES #21).

Evano first appeared in EVANO THE TERRIBLE (JUSTICE LEAGUE ADVENTURES #18).

The Flash first appeared on JUSTICE LEAGUE in SECRET ORIGINS, Part One (Episode #1).

Green Lantern John Stewart first appeared in SECRET ORIGINS, Part One (Episode #1).

The Green Lantern Corps first appeared on JUSTICE LEAGUE in IN BLACKEST NIGHT, Part One (Episode #4).

Hawkgirl first appeared in SECRET ORIGINS, Part One (Episode #1).

Hippolyta first appeared in SECRET ORIGINS, Part One (Episode #1).

Icicle first appeared in COLD WAR (JUSTICE LEAGUE ADVENTURES #12).

The Joker first appeared on JUSTICE LEAGUE in INJUSTICE FOR ALL, Part One (Episode #8).

J'onn J'onnz, the Martian Manhunter, first appeared in SECRET ORIGINS, Part One (Episode #1).

Killer Frost first appeared in COLD WAR (JUSTICE LEAGUE ADVENTURES #12).

Kobra first appeared in VENOMOUS AGENDA (JUSTICE LEAGUE ADVENTURES #23).

Lady Eve first appeared in VENOMOUS

AGENDA (JUSTICE LEAGUE ADVENTURES #23).

Lex Luthor first appeared on JUSTICE LEAGUE in INJUSTICE FOR ALL, Part One (Episode #8).

Mercy Graves first appeared on JUSTICE LEAGUE in TABULA RASA, Part One (Episode #29).

Minister Blizzard first appeared in COLD WAR (JUSTICE LEAGUE ADVENTURES #12).

Mr. Freeze appeared in COLD WAR (JUSTICE LEAGUE ADVENTURES #12)

Poison Ivy appeared in AN ANGRY TIDE (JUSTICE LEAGUE ADVENTURES #14)

Polar Lord (a.k.a. Eklu) first appeared in COLD WAR (JUSTICE LEAGUE ADVENTURES #12).

Psycho-Pirate first appeared in EMOTIONAL BAGGAGE (JUSTICE LEAGUE ADVENTURES #20).

The Shade first appeared in INJUSTICE FOR ALL, Part One (Episode #8).

The Shayol first appeared in SECOND CONTACT (JUSTICE LEAGUE ADVENTURES #22).

Snowman first appeared in COLD WAR (JUSTICE LEAGUE ADVENTURES #12)

Solomon Grundy first appeared in INJUSTICE FOR ALL, Part One (Episode #8).

Star Sapphire first appeared in INJUSTICE FOR ALL, Part One (Episode #8).

Starro appeared in THE STAR-CONQUEROR (JUSTICE LEAGUE ADVENTURES #5).

Superman first appeared on JUSTICE LEAGUE in SECRET ORIGINS, Part One (Episode #1).

The Ultra-Humanite first appeared in INJUSTICE FOR ALL, Part One (Episode #8).

Wonder Woman first appeared in SECRET ORIGINS, Part One (Episode #1).

Index

ACKNOWLEDGMENTS

Dorling Kindersley would like to thank the following DC artists for their contributions to this book:

Christian Alamy, Aluir Amancio, Rick Burchett, Dan Davis, John Delaney, Randy Elliott, Wayne Faucher, Chris Jones, Min S. Ku, Rob Leigh, Tim Levins, David Lopez, Al Nickerson, Mark Propst, Robin Riggs, Craig Rousseau, John K. Snyder, and Joe Staton.

The author would like to thank the following people:

Edward T. Tonai, the fine folks at Toon Zone (especially Joseph, James, and Jim), Samuel Demich (the real Batman), Chris Cerasi, Steve Korté, and all the talented people behind the Justice League Animated series, comics, and books.

Dorling Kindersley would like to thank:
Steve Korté and Chris Cerasi at DC Comics.